First World War
and Army of Occupation
War Diary
France, Belgium and Germany

37 DIVISION
Divisional Troops
Prince of Wales's (North Staffordshire Regiment)
9 Battalion (Maps)

WO95/2524/2

The Naval & Military Press Ltd
www.nmarchive.com
Published in association with The National Archives

Published by

The Naval & Military Press Ltd

Unit 10 Ridgewood Industrial Park,

Uckfield, East Sussex,

TN22 5QE England

Tel: +44 (0) 1825 749494

www.naval-military-press.com

www.nmarchive.com

This diary has been reprinted in facsimile from the original. Any imperfections are inevitably reproduced and the quality may fall short of modern type and cartographic standards.

© **Crown Copyright**
Images reproduced by permission of The National Archives, London, England, 2015.

Contents

Document type	Place/Title	Date From	Date To
Heading	Maps Belonging 98th North Staffs Diary (Loose In Box)		
Diagram etc			
Map			
Heading	War Diary 9th North Stafford Regt September		
Map			
Miscellaneous	War Diary 9th North Staffs October 1917		
Diagram etc	Trenches Corrected To 22.12.17		
Map			
Heading	War Diary November 1917 9th North Staffs.		
Map			
Heading	Appendix to Feb 1918 War Diary 9th North Stafford Regt.		
Map			
Heading	France Sheet 57B 51A 51 1/40000 Shewing Work On Roads During November 1918		
Map			
Map	France		
Map	Sheet 5		
Map			
Map	France		
Miscellaneous			

MAPS BELONGING
9 BTN NORTH STAFFS DIARY
(LOOSE IN BOX)

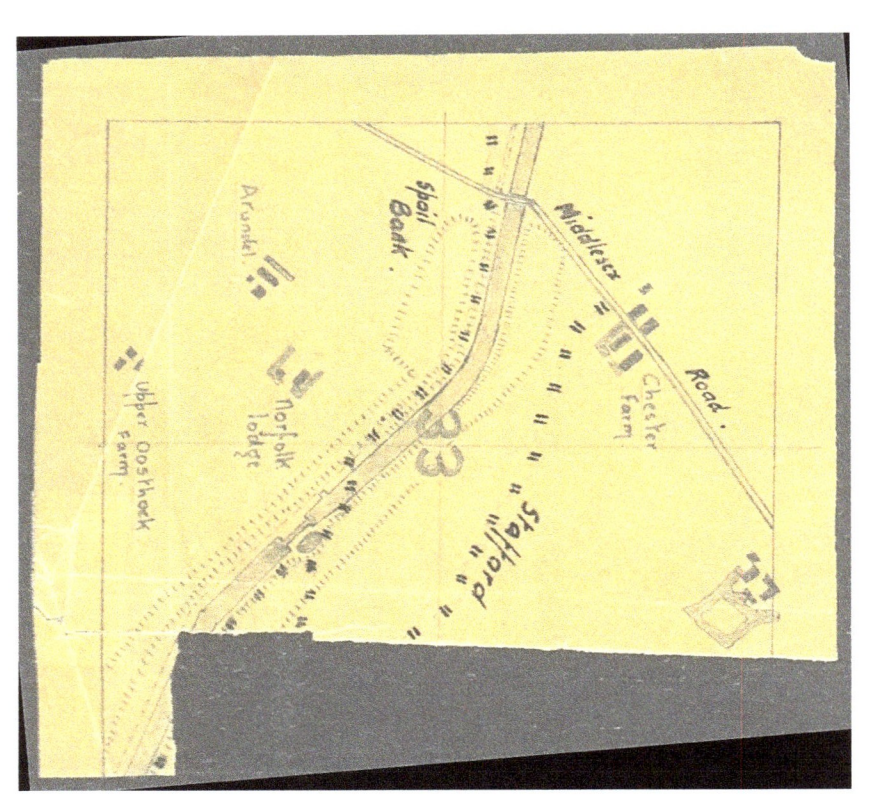

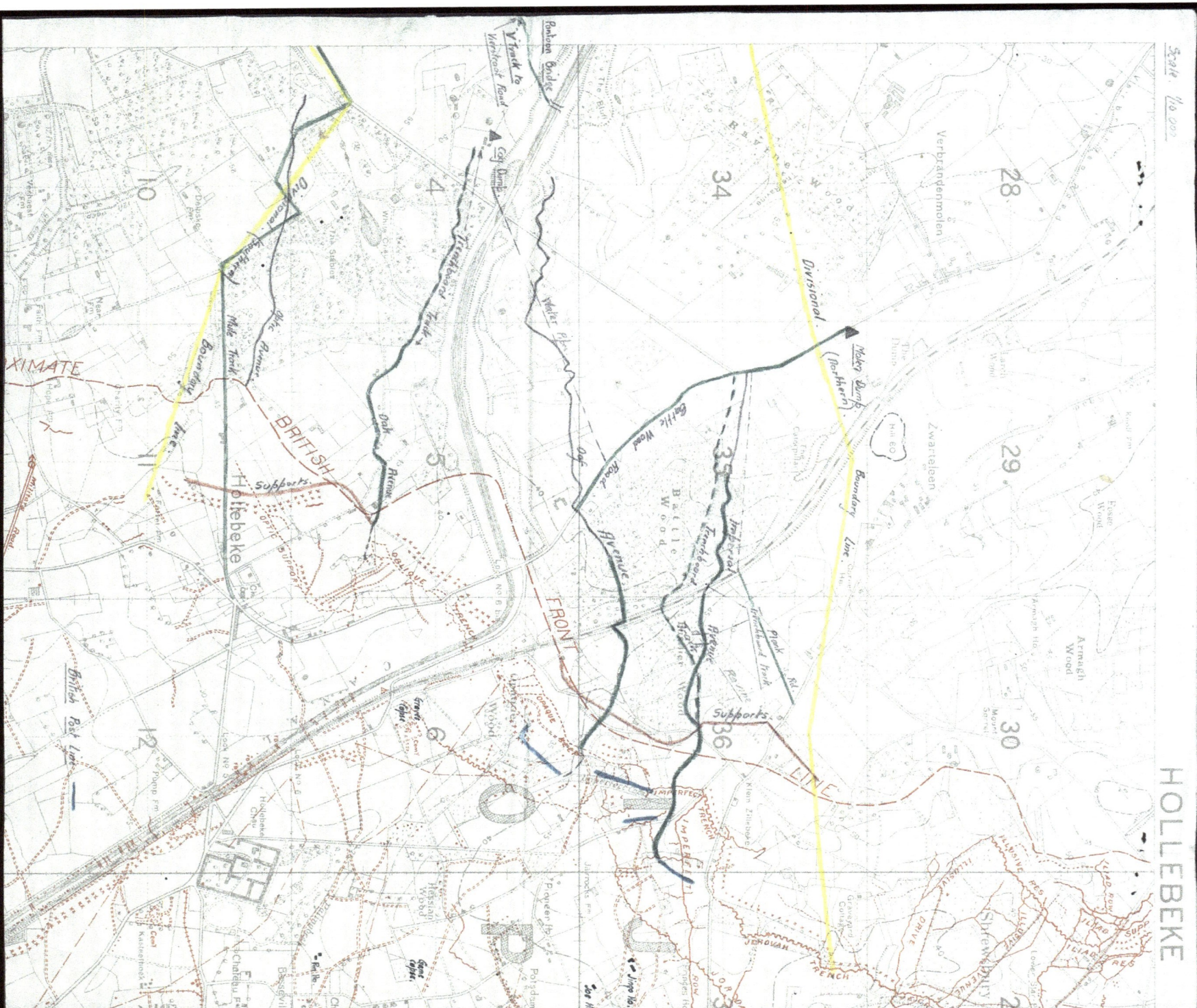

War Diary.
9th North Stafford Regt.
September.

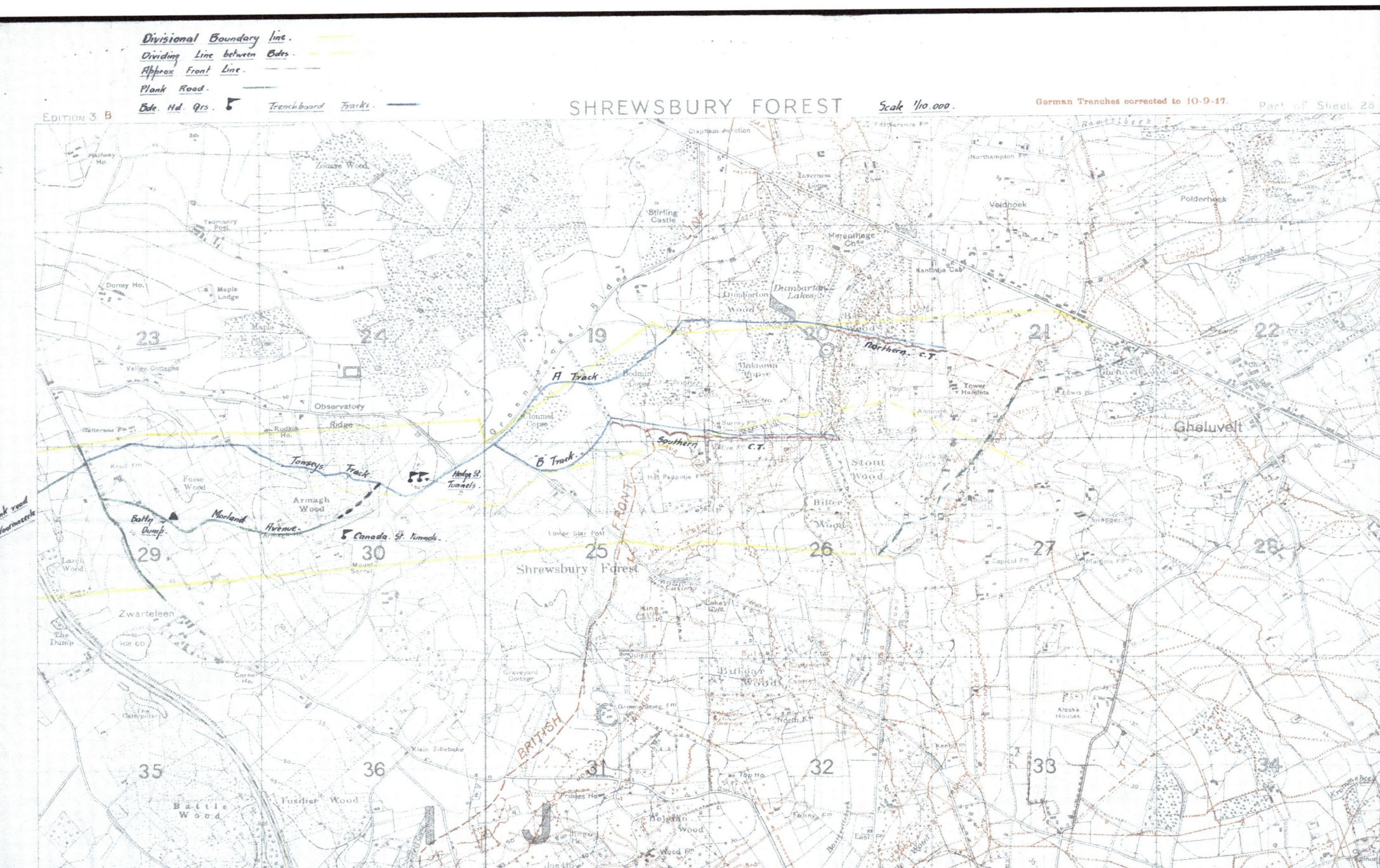

War Diary.
9th North Staffs.
October, 1917.

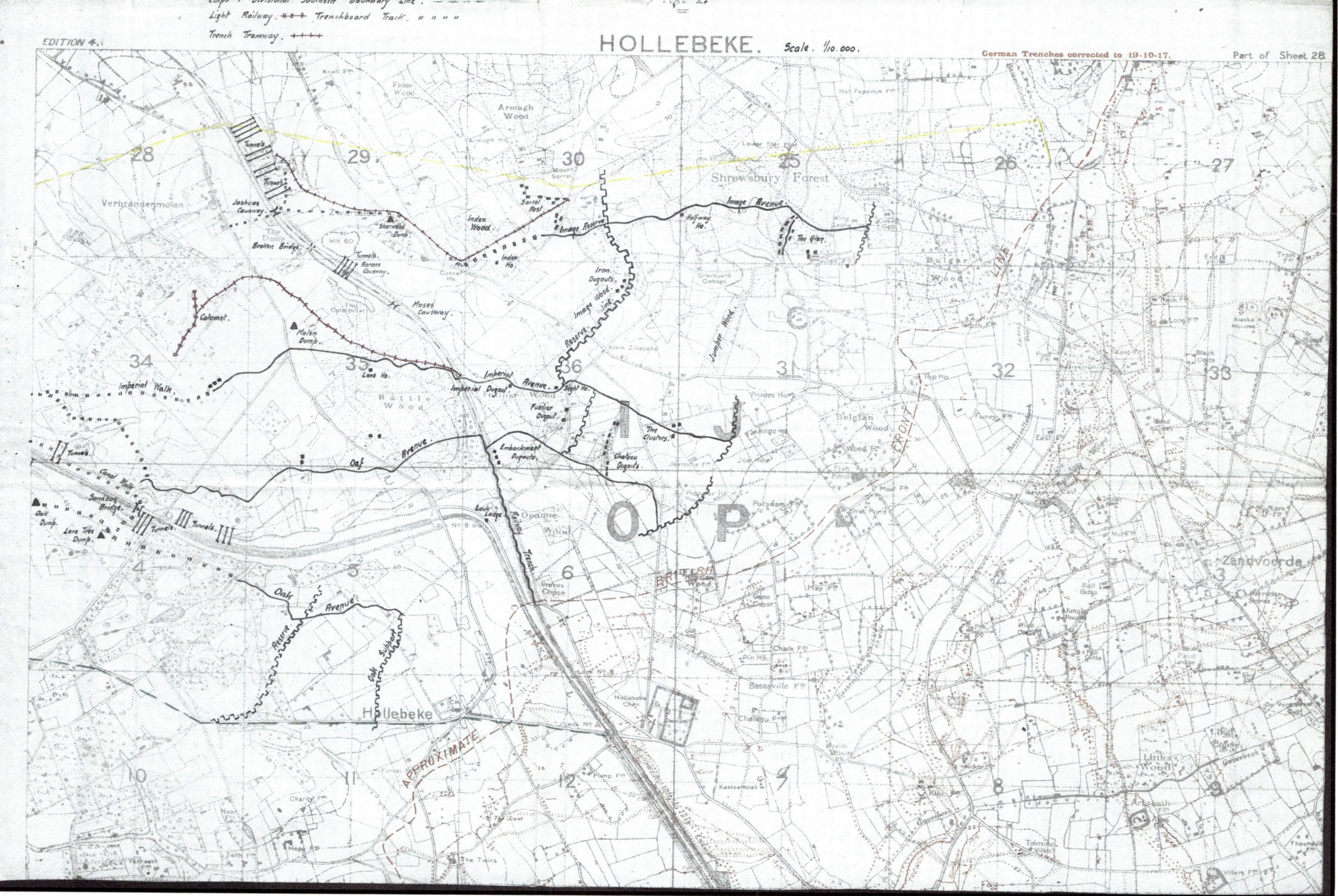

War Diary
November 1917
9th North Staff.

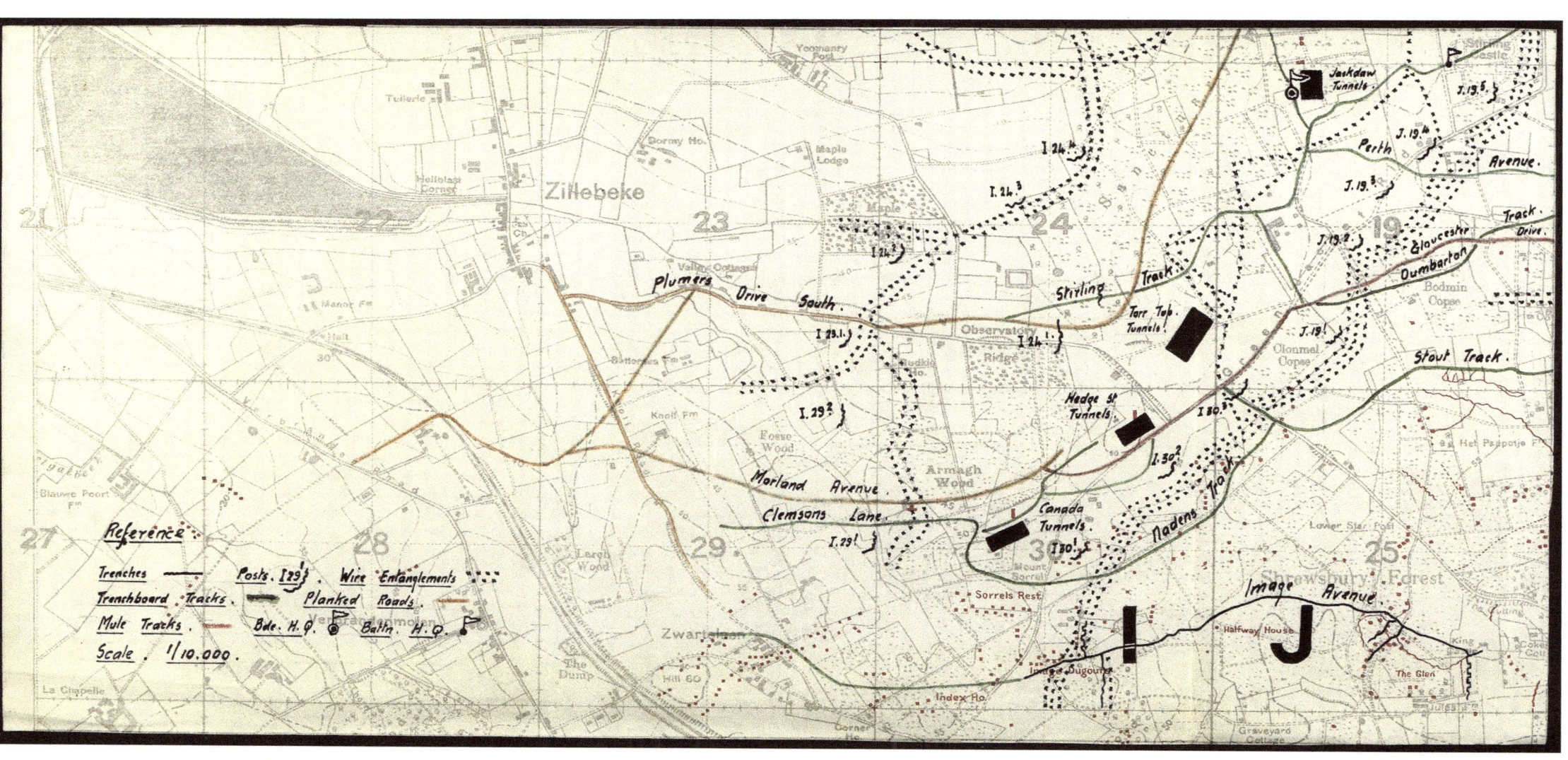

Appendix X Feb 1918.
War Diary
9th North Stafford Regt.

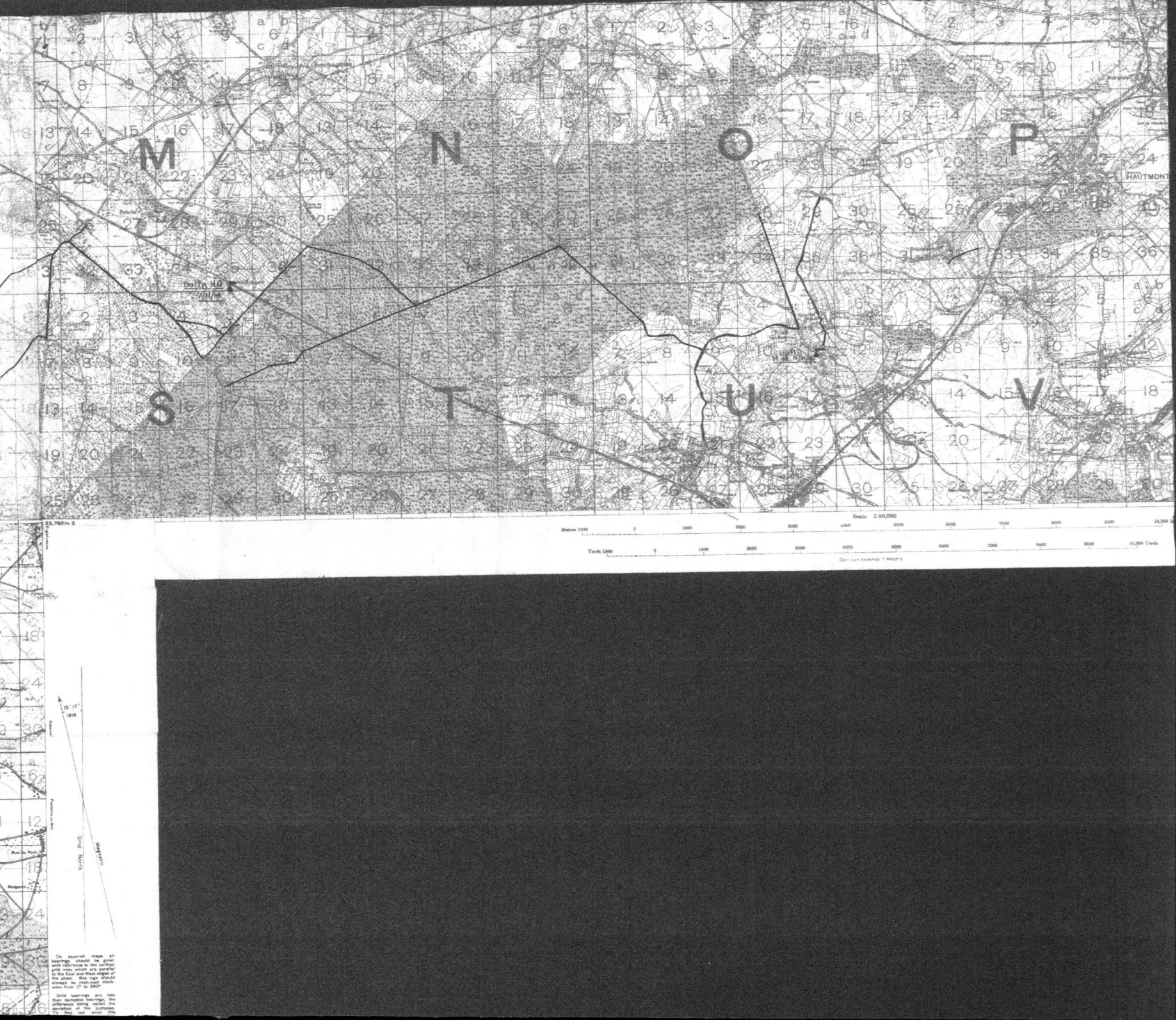

FRANCE

SHEETS 57S, 51Q, 51

1/40000

SHEWING WORK ON

ROADS DURING

NOVEMBER 1918

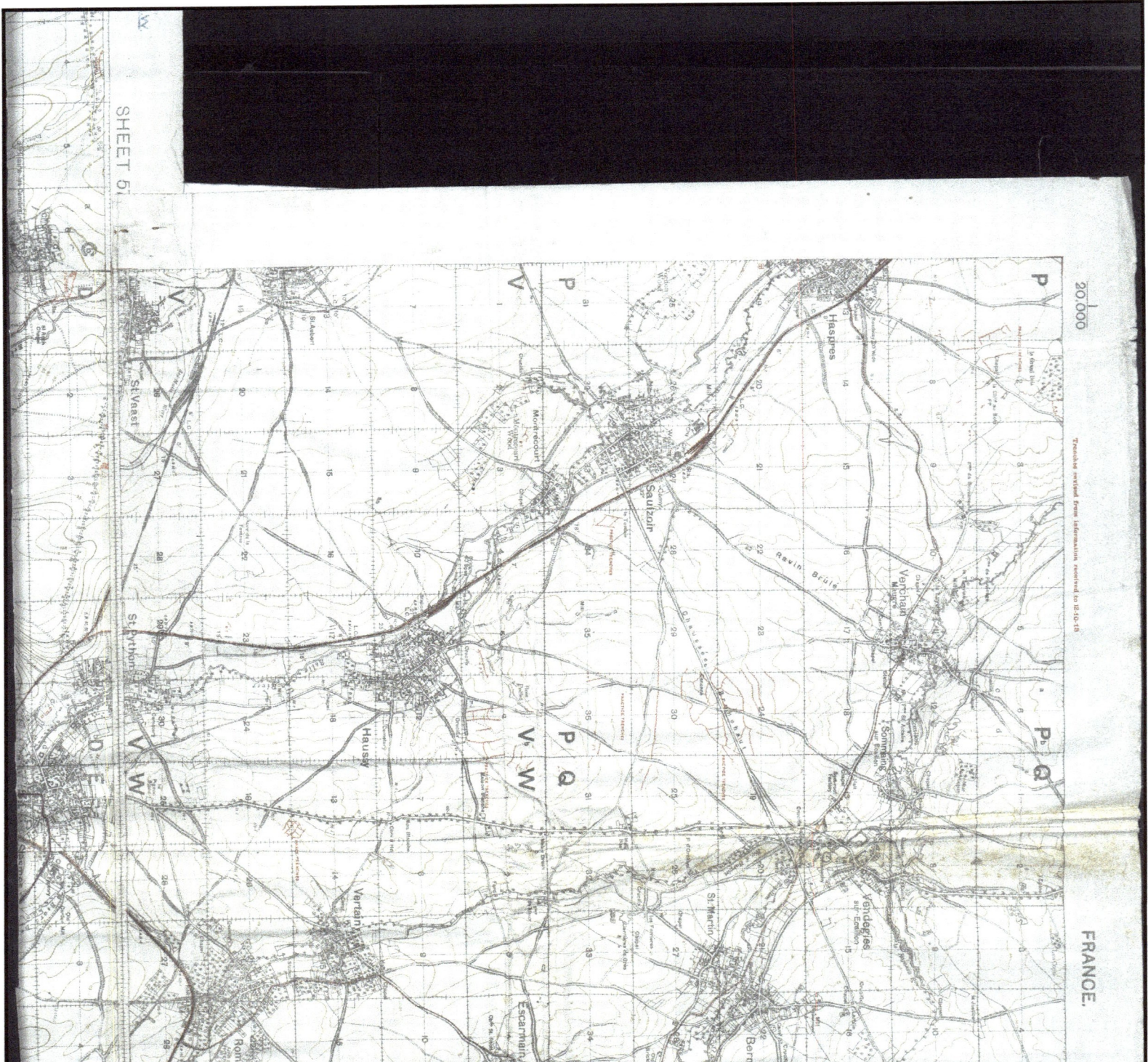

FRANCE.

EDITION 3a

SHEET 51/A S.E.

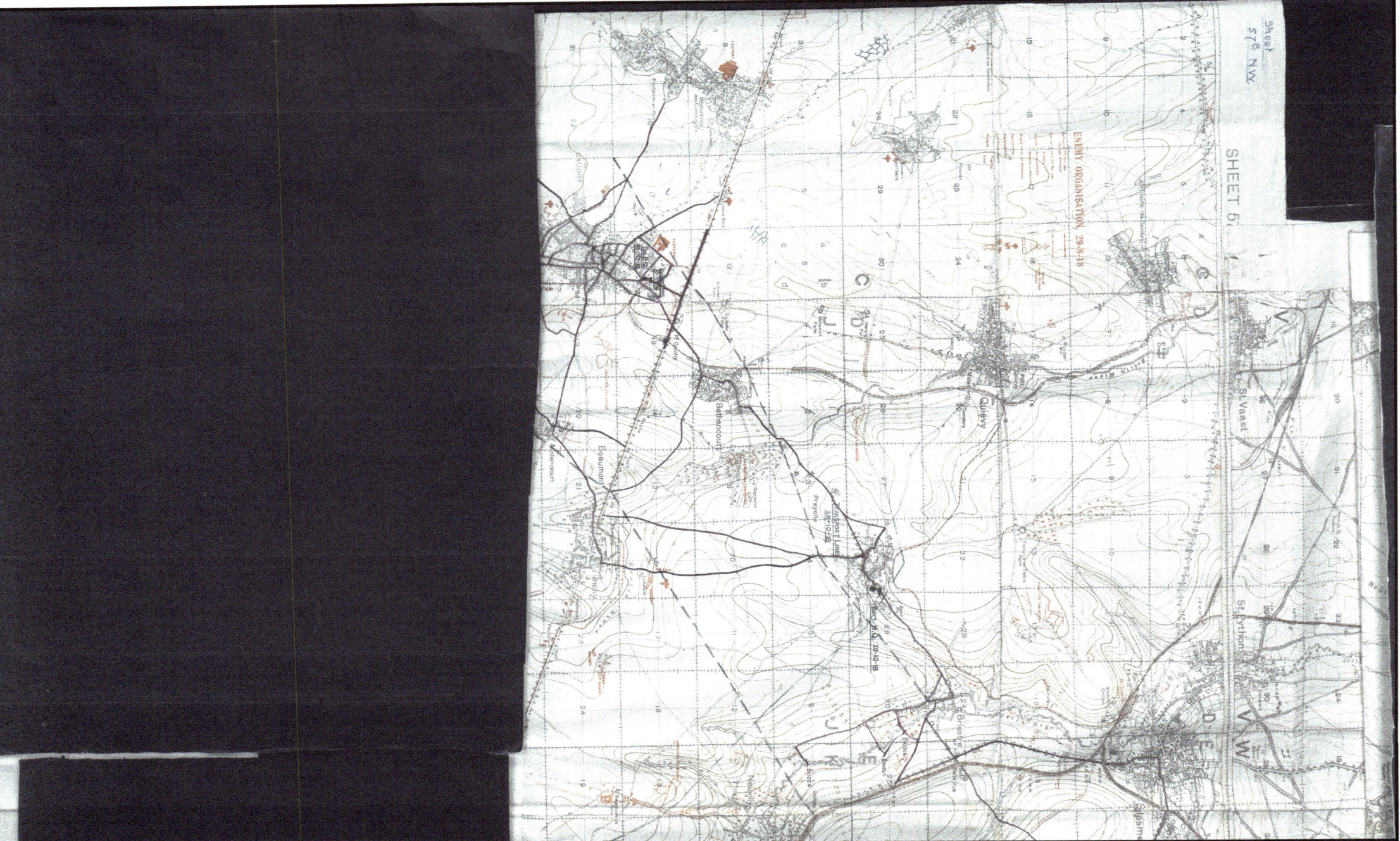

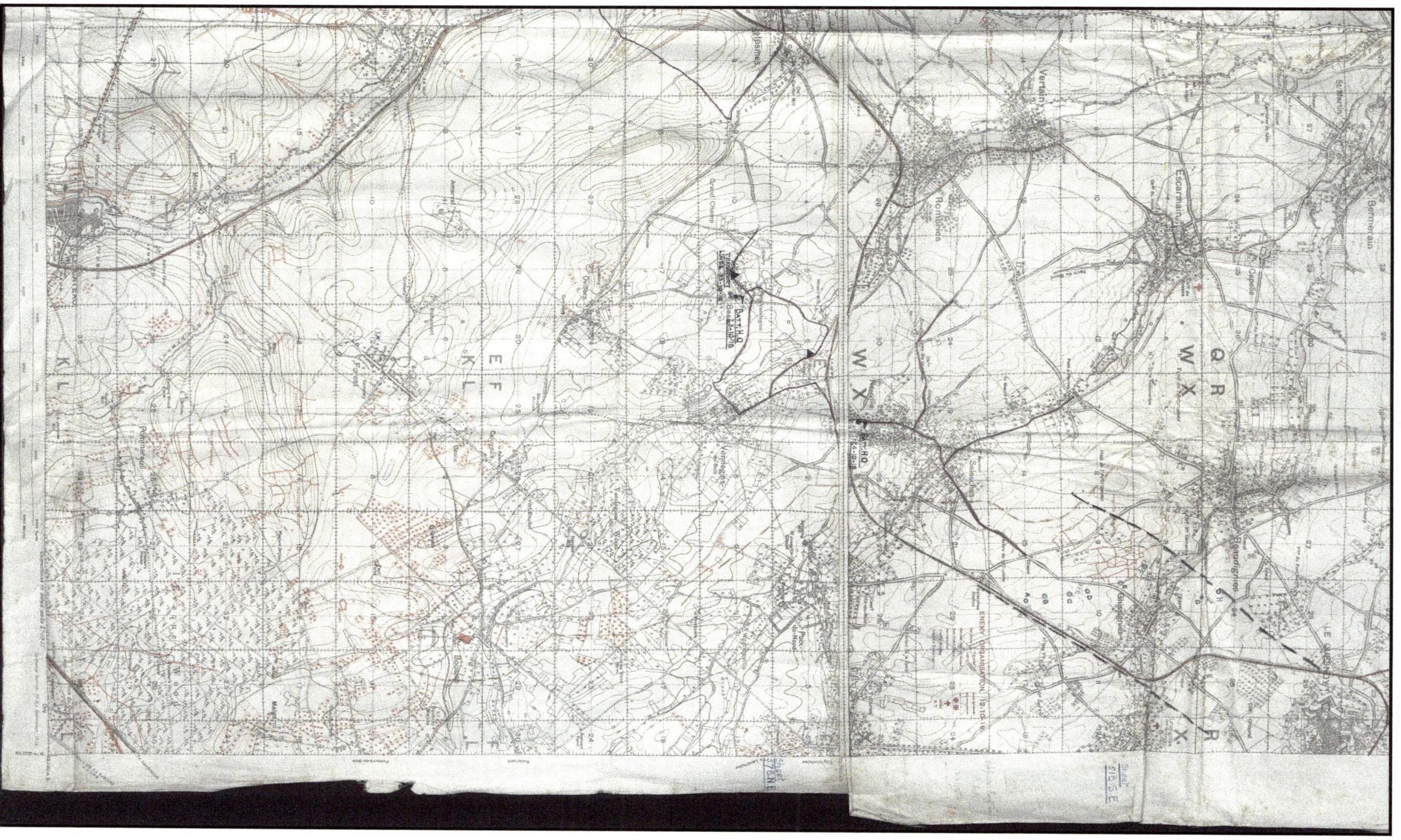

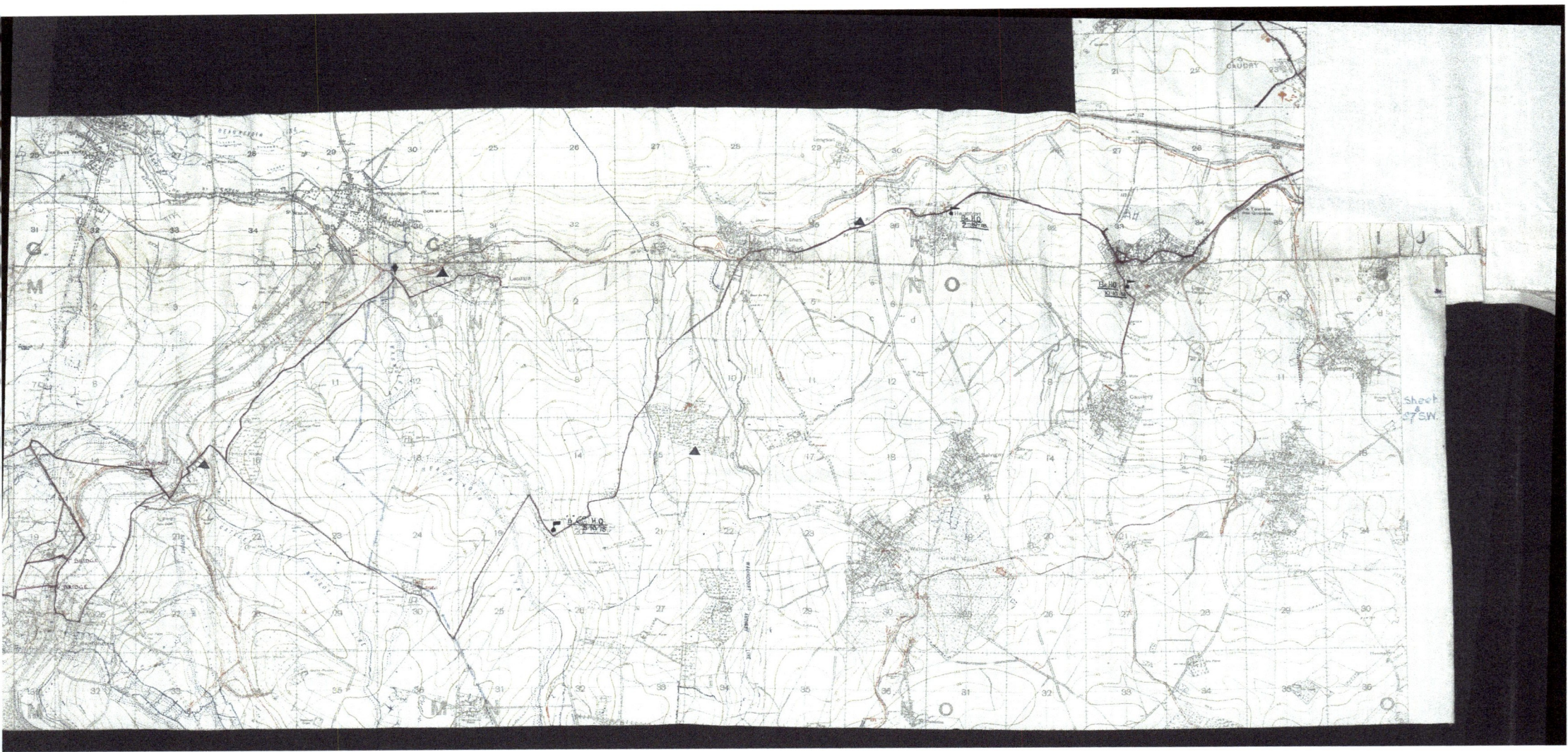

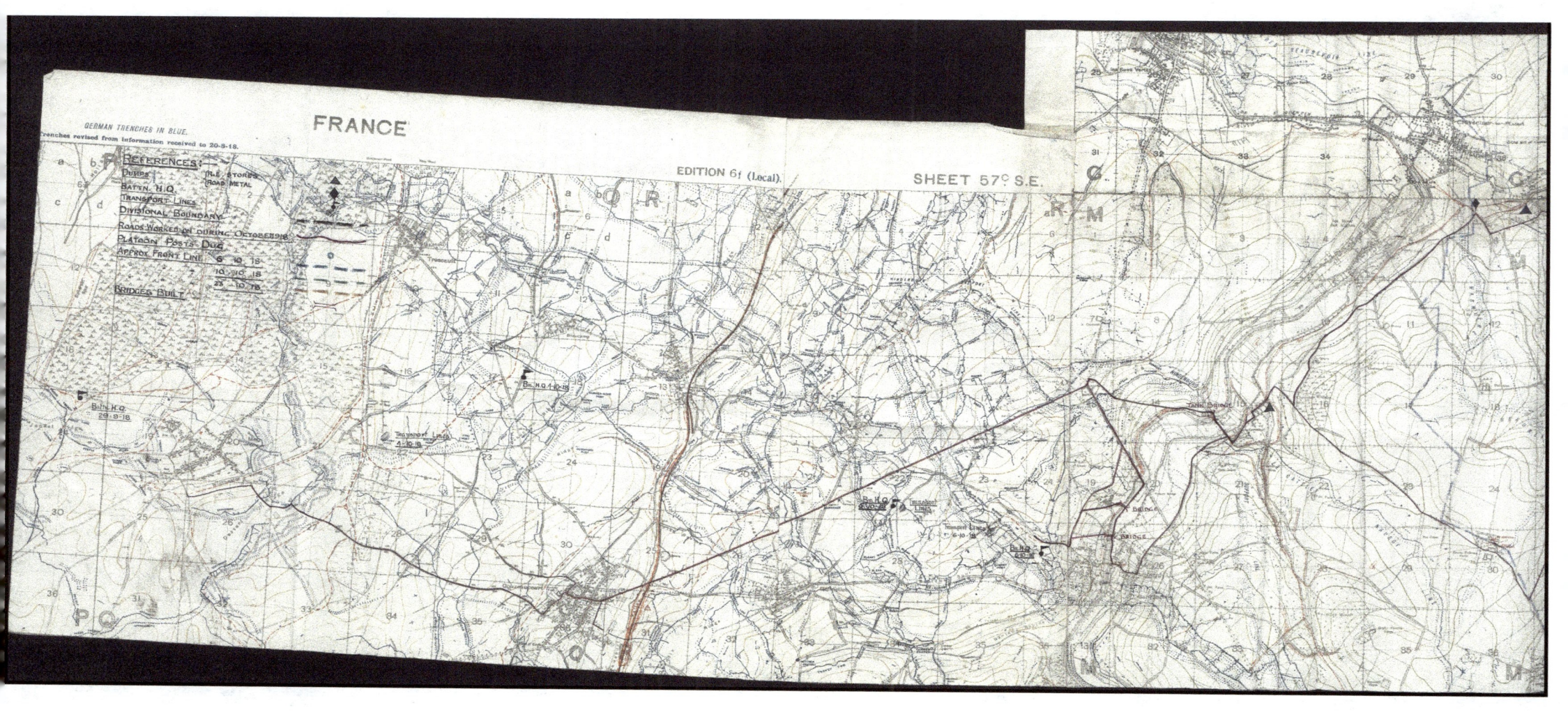

www.ingramcontent.com/pod-product-compliance
Lightning Source LLC
Chambersburg PA
CBHW081251170426
43191CB00037B/2114

9781474518116